THE IRISH GET UP AND

ISBN 978-1-068237

Get Up & Go

Tús maith leath na hoibre.
A good start is half the work

Get Up and Go Publications
WE ASPIRE TO INSPIRE

Published in Ireland by

GET UP AND GO PUBLICATIONS LTD

Unit 7A Cornhill Business Complex, Ballyshannon, Co Donegal, F94 C4AA.
Email: info@getupandgodiary.com
www.getupandgodiary.com

Compiled by the Get Up and Go team
Graphic Design by Rosie Gray
Illustrations: freepik.com
Printed in Ireland by GPS Colour Graphics

2026 BANK AND PUBLIC HOLIDAYS

REPUBLIC OF IRELAND

New Year's Day, 1 January	St Brigid's Day, 2 February
St. Patricks Day, 17 March	Good Friday, 3 April
Easter Monday, 6 April	May Day Bank Holiday, 4 May
June Bank Holiday, 1 June	August Bank Holiday, 3 August
October Bank Holiday, 26 October	Christmas Day, 25 December
St Stephen's Day, 26 December*	Bank Holiday, 28 December*

NORTHERN IRELAND

New Year's Day, 1 January	St. Patricks Day, 17 March
Good Friday, 3 April	Easter Monday, 6 April
May Day Bank Holiday, 4 May	Spring Bank Holiday, 25 May
Orangeman's Holiday. 13 July	Summer Bank Holiday, 31 August
Christmas Day, 25 December	Boxing Day, 26 December*
Bank Holiday, 28 December*	

ENGLAND, SCOTLAND AND WALES

New Year's Day, 1 January	2 January, Scotland
Good Friday, 3 April	Easter Monday, 6 April
St George's Day, 23 April	May Bank Holiday, 4 May
Spring Bank Holiday, 25 May	Summer Bank Holiday, 3 August
Late Summer Bank Holiday, 31 August	Remembrance Day, 11 November
St Andrews Day, 30 November	Christmas Day, 25 December
Boxing Day, 26 December*	Bank Holiday, 28 December*

USA

New Year's Day, 1 January	Martin Luther King Jr. Day, 19 January
Presidents' Day, 16 February	Memorial Day, 25 May
Independence Day, 3 July?	Labor Day, 7 September
Columbus Day, 12 October	Veteran's Day, 11 November
Thanksgiving Day, 26 November	Christmas Day' 25 December

CANADA

New Year's Day, 1 January	Family Day, 16 February
Commonwealth Day, 9 March	St. Patricks Day, 17 March
Good Friday, 3 April	Easter Monday, 6 April
Victoria Day, 18 May	Canada Day, 1 July
Civic Day, 3 August	Labour Day, 7 September
Thanksgiving Day, 12 October	Remembrance Day, 11 November
Christmas Day, 25 December	Boxing Day, 26 December*
Bank Holiday, 28 December*	

AUSTRALIA HOLIDAYS

New Year's Day, 1 January	Australia Day. 26 January
Good Friday, 3 April	Easter Monday, 6 April
Anzac Day, 25 April	King's Birthday, 8 June
Boxing Day, 26 December	Bank Holiday, 28 December

2026 CALENDAR

January

S	M	T	W	T	F	S
				1	2	3
4	5	6	7	8	9	10
11	12	13	14	15	16	17
18	19	20	21	22	23	24
25	26	27	28	29	30	31

February

S	M	T	W	T	F	S
1	2	3	4	5	6	7
8	9	10	11	12	13	14
15	16	17	18	19	20	21
22	23	24	25	26	27	28

March

S	M	T	W	T	F	S
1	2	3	4	5	6	7
8	9	10	11	12	13	14
15	16	17	18	19	20	21
22	23	24	25	26	27	28
29	30	31				

April

S	M	T	W	T	F	S
			1	2	3	4
5	6	7	8	9	10	11
12	13	14	15	16	17	18
19	20	21	22	23	24	25
26	27	28	29	30		

May

S	M	T	W	T	F	S
					1	2
3	4	5	6	7	8	9
10	11	12	13	14	15	16
17	18	19	20	21	22	23
24	25	26	27	28	29	30
31						

June

S	M	T	W	T	F	S
	1	2	3	4	5	6
7	8	9	10	11	12	13
14	15	16	17	18	19	20
21	22	23	24	25	26	27
28	29	30				

July

S	M	T	W	T	F	S
			1	2	3	4
5	6	7	8	9	10	11
12	13	14	15	16	17	18
19	20	21	22	23	24	25
26	27	28	29	30	31	

August

S	M	T	W	T	F	S
						1
2	3	4	5	6	7	8
9	10	11	12	13	14	15
16	17	18	19	20	21	22
23	24	25	26	27	28	29
30	31					

September

S	M	T	W	T	F	S
		1	2	3	4	5
6	7	8	9	10	11	12
13	14	15	16	17	18	19
20	21	22	23	24	25	26
27	28	29	30			

October

S	M	T	W	T	F	S
				1	2	3
4	5	6	7	8	9	10
11	12	13	14	15	16	17
18	19	20	21	22	23	24
25	26	27	28	29	30	31

November

S	M	T	W	T	F	S
1	2	3	4	5	6	7
8	9	10	11	12	13	14
15	16	17	18	19	20	21
22	23	24	25	26	27	28
29	30					

December

S	M	T	W	T	F	S
		1	2	3	4	5
6	7	8	9	10	11	12
13	14	15	16	17	18	19
20	21	22	23	24	25	26
27	28	29	30	31		

FORGIVE THE PAST - LET IT GO
LIVE THE PRESENT - THE POWER OF NOW
CREATE THE FUTURE - THOUGHTS BECOME THINGS

A Chara/Dear Friend,

Welcome to the 2026 edition of the Get Up and Go Diary!

Whether you're a first-time user or one of our loyal readers, thank you for choosing this inspirational diary. Whether it's a personal purchase or a thoughtful gift, we hope it fills your days with motivation, insight, and encouragement.

Use your diary as a daily planner or a journaling tool. Journaling helps you reflect, set goals, track progress, and stay focused — a powerful practice for personal growth.

Each purchase makes a difference. A portion of every diary sold supports impactful causes in the developing world through our partnership with **B1G1 – Business for Good** (www.B1G1.com). Our paper is sourced from **FSC-certified suppliers**, ensuring it comes from legal and sustainable forests (https://fsc.org).

We're proud to be accredited for the **seventh year running** by the All-Ireland Business Foundation as a Best in Class Inspirational Publication (www.AIBF.ie).

To explore our full range, buy additional copies, or subscribe to our newsletter, visit **www.getupandgodiary.com**. Stay connected through our community and enjoy early access to new products and discounts. (See order form page 148).

Follow us online:

- Facebook: The Irish Get Up and Go Diary
- Twitter: @getupandgo1
- Instagram: @getupandgodiaries

Love the diary? Share it with your friends and family!

Best wishes for 2026!

Slán go fóill/Bye for now

From the team at Get Up and Go Publications Ltd

This diary belongs to: _____

Address:_____

Tel: _____ Email: _____

Emergency Telephone Number: _____

SPRIOCANNA
GOALS FOR JANUARY
EANÁIR

_____

_____

_____

_____

_____

_____

_____

_____

_____

_____

_____

Faigh ainm duine a éiríonn go luath agus is féidir leat codladh ar feadh an lae.

Get the name of an early riser and you can sleep all day.

An Irish Quote

If you greatly desire something, Have the guts to stake everything on obtaining it.
Brendan Behan

Being Irish is very much a part of who I am. I take it everywhere with me.
Colin Farrell

January

A 2026 WISH FOR YOU

12 months of Joy   52 weeks of Laughter   365 days of Peace

Get Up and Go team

The Months Ahead

January brings the snow, makes our feet and fingers glow.
February brings the rain, Thaws the frozen lake again.
March brings breezes loud and shrill, stirs the dancing daffodil.
April brings the primrose sweet, Scatters daises at our feet.
May brings flocks of pretty lambs, Skipping by their fleecy damns.
June brings tulips, lilies, roses, Fills the children's hand with posies.
Hot July brings cooling showers, Apricots and gillyflowers.
August brings the sheaves of corn, Then the harvest home is borne.
Warm September brings the fruit, Sportsmen then begin to shoot.
Fresh October brings the pheasants, Then to gather nuts is pleasant.
Dull November brings the blast,
Then the leaves are whirling fast.
Chill December brings the sleet,
Blazing fire, and Christmas treat.

By Sara Coleridge

Attitudes are our secret power working twenty-four hours a day, for good or bad. It is of paramount importance that we know how to harness and control this great force.

Tom Blandi

Thursday **01**

Carpe Diem

Friday **02**

Get Up And Go for 2026

Full Moon, Wolf Moon   Saturday **03**

Let go of the past

Sunday **04**

Remember people's birthdays - start a birthday book

Look at everything as though you were seeing it either for the first or last time.

Betty Smith

January

It's not what you do some of the time, it's what you do most of the time that makes the difference.

Tom Crean

Excellence is not a skill it's an attitude.

Ralph Marston

Monday **05**

Cultivate the habit of expecting good things

Tuesday **06**   Women's little Christmas

Your attitude controls your life

Wednesday **07**

Opportunity can knock very softly

Thursday **08**

If you don't like it change it

Friday **09**

Walk the extra mile

Saturday **10**

We don't have problems, we have challenges

Sunday **11**

Life is a series of lessons to be learned

A person with a new idea is a crank until the idea succeeds.

Mark Twain

The winds of change are always blowing.

January

Confusion is the first step towards wisdom. Folly is thinking that you have all the answers.

Neale Donald Walsch

If you can't get rid of the skeleton in your closet, you'd best take it out and teach it to dance.

George Bernard Shaw

Monday **12**

Sharing is caring

Tuesday **13**

All your future lies ahead

Wednesday **14**

The best is yet to come...

Thursday 15

Mind your own business

Friday 16

Plan your course of action

Saturday 17

Believe in miracles

New Moon **Sunday 18**

Do not waste time crossing bridges you have not reached

Be hard on the issue, soft on the person.
Henry Cloud

Don't look for yourself, create yourself.

January

There is only one way to avoid criticism: Do nothing, say nothing, and be nothing.

Aristotle

You are your thoughts, Change them and you change your life.

Monday **19**

Organise your workspace

Tuesday **20**

Every action is a feeling expressed

Wednesday **21**

Where there's a will, there's a way

Thursday 22

In a gentle way, you can shake the world

Friday 23

If you fear something go out and do it

Saturday 24

Follow your instincts

Sunday 25

Choose never to be a prisoner of urgency

Make people feel important with the SHR method: Seen, Heard, Remembered.

Ben Meer

Forgive the past. Live the present. Create the future.

January

A good laugh and a long sleep are the two best cures for anything.

Irish proverb

Don't be discouraged. It's often the last key in the bunch that opens the lock.

Unknown

Monday **26**

Be a player not a spectator

Tuesday **27**

Don't react, take time to respond

Wednesday **28**

Start your new healthy breakfast trend

Thursday **29**

Knowing is the enemy of learning

Friday **30**

Make that appointment for a health check

Saturday **31**

Be daring / be different

If you are DEPRESSED, you are living in the PAST
If you are ANXIOUS, you are living in the FUTURE.
If you are at PEACE, you are living in the PRESENT

Lao Tzu

Nothing can dim the light that shines from within

Maya Angelou

The Night Of Women's Christmas:

January 6th-7th 1839

Was the Night of the Big Wind affecting all of Ireland, Scotland, Wales, Northern England

There was fury in the storm that came last night
last night, the Christmas of Women;
as if released from a distant bedlam
a lunatic shriek through the sky;
rattling against the gate like the gaggling of geese
roaring up the river like a bellowing bull
dousing my candle like a blow upon my mouth: -
an unexpected spark for anger.

I hope such a storm will come to me
The night I begin to die
As I return home from the dance of life
with the light of this life failing,
so every moment might be filled with cries from the sky,
transforming the world into a chorus of screams,
so I would not hear the silence moving toward me
or feel the engine that moves me stop.

Seán Ó Ríordáin translated into English

Your Greatest Power Is The Power To Be

To be loving.
To be courageous.
To be joyful.
To be friendly.
To be kind.
To be aware.
To be forgiving.
To be tolerant.
To be patient.
To be humble.
To be helpful.
To be there.
To be a great human being.

Get up and go diary 2026

SPRIOCANNA

FEABHRA

_____
_____
_____
_____
_____
_____
_____
_____
_____
_____
_____

An Irish Quote
*Our greatest glory is not in
never falling,
But rising every time we fall.*
Oliver Goldsmith

*Beart gan leigheas,
foighne is fearr dó.*

Patience is the best
thing for an incurable
situation.

May the hinges of our friendship never grow rusty.
Irish saying

February

You Raise Me Up

When I am down and, oh, my soul, so weary.
When troubles come and my heart burdened be.
Then I am still and wait here in the silence,
Until you come and sit awhile with me.

You raise me up, so I can stand on mountains.
You raise me up to walk on stormy seas.
I am strong when I am on your shoulders.
You raise me up to more than I can be.

There is no life - no life without its hunger.
Each restless heart beats so imperfectly.
But when you come and I am filled with wonder,
Sometimes, I think I glimpse eternity.

You raise me up, so I can stand on mountains.
You raise me up to walk on stormy seas.
I am strong when I am on your shoulders.
You raise me up to more than I can be.

Brendan Graham

Grandma Always Said

Don't go where you're not invited.
Don't talk about what you don't know
Don't interfere with things that are none of your business
Don't open cupboard or fridge doors in other people's houses.
Don't go to see people at lunchtime
Don't call to people after 10pm
Don't go into anyone's bedroom without permission.
Good manners are easy carried and never go out of fashion.

That's not my job

This is a story about four people named Everybody, Somebody, Anybody and Nobody. There was an important job to be done, and Everybody thought Somebody would do it. Anybody could have done it, but Nobody did it. Somebody got angry that, because it was Everybody's job.
Everybody thought Anybody could do it, but Nobody realised that Everybody wouldn't do it. It ended up that Everybody blamed Somebody when Nobody did what Anybody could have done.

Unknown

It doesn't matter who you are, where you come from. The ability to triumph begins with you – always.

Oprah Winfrey

One day a man was walking along the beach, when he noticed a boy picking something up and gently throwing it into the ocean. Approaching the boy, he asked, "What are you doing?" The youth replied, "Throwing starfish back into the ocean. The surf is up, and the tide is going out. If I don't throw them back, they'll die." "Son," the man said, "don't you realize there are miles and miles of beach and hundreds of starfish? You can't make a difference!" After listening politely, the boy bent down, picked up another starfish, and threw it back into the surf. Then, smiling at the man, he said…"I made a difference for that one."

Adapted from original story by Loren Eiseley

Full Moon, Snow Moon	Sunday **01**

All is well in your world

February

Meeting you was fate
Becoming your friend was a choice.
But falling in LOVE with you was
beyond my CONTROL.
If I did anything right in my life,
I give my heart to you.
I wish I could turn back the clock.
I'd find you sooner. And get to LOVE you longer.

Monday **02**   St Brigid's Day

Pay off your credit cards every month

Tuesday **03**

Look for a new, joyous feeling within you

Wednesday **04**

Cultivate your unique, natural self

Thursday 05

Let go of rigid plans and concepts

Friday 06

See wholeness in place of good and bad fortune

Saturday 07

Gather as much virtue as you possibly can

Sunday 08

Examine your habits

People will love you. People will hate you. And none of it will have anything to do with you.

Abraham Hicks

February

Those we love can never be more than a thought away, for as long as there's a memory they live in our hearts to stay.

The only place where success comes before work is in the dictionary.

Vidal Sassoon

Monday 09

However good or bad a situation is, it will change

Tuesday 10

Don't take yourself so seriously. No one else does

Wednesday 11

Have a happy mind

Thursday **12**

True freedom lies in choice

Friday **13**

Be strong by bending

Happy Valentine's Day

Saturday **14**

Let your day be full of love

Sunday **15**

Get outside every day, miracles are waiting everywhere

Everything in your life is a reflection of a choice you made, If you want a different result, make a different choice.

Anonymous

February

If you want to know your past life, look at your present condition. If you want to know your future life, look at your present actions.

Padmasambhava

When entrusted with a secret, keep it.

Monday 16

No one is responsible for your happiness but you

Tuesday 17

New Moon
Pancake Tuesday

You cannot be lonely if you like the person, you are alone with

---

Wednesday 18

Ash Wednesday

Dieting is a losing battle

Thursday **19**

When in doubt, just take the next small step

Friday **20**

Perhaps what you are looking for is right in front of you

Saturday **21**

Make peace with your past so it won't mess up the present

Sunday **22**

Take some deep breaths, it calms the mind

Prayer is the voice of longing; it reaches outwards and inwards to unearth our ancient belonging.

John O'Donohue

February

There is no such thing as a bad day, just bad moments that we insist on carrying all day long!

After writing an angry email or text, read it carefully. Then delete it.

Nixon Waterman

Monday **23**

Over prepare, then go with the flow

Tuesday **24**

Your health is your wealth

Wednesday **25**

Do the difficult things while they are easy

Thursday **26**

Charity begins at home

Friday **27**

The point of power is always in the present moment

Saturday **28**

Appointments for a health check take time, make one tomorrow

If I Knew You

If I knew you and you knew me,
If both of us could clearly see,
And with an inner sight divine,
The meaning of your heart and
mine,
I'm sure that we would differ less,
And clasp our hands in friendliness;
Our thoughts would pleasantly
agree,
If I knew you and you knew me.

Nixon Waterman

SPRIOCANNA MÁRTA

GOALS FOR MARCH

For each petal on the shamrock, this brings a wish your way: Good health, good luck, and happiness for today and every day.

Irish blessing

Beatha teanga í a labhairt.

The life of a language is to speak it.

Every St. Patrick's Day every Irishman goes out to find another Irishman to make a speech to.

Shane Leslie

Some Good Auld Irish Sayings

"The craic was ninety"

"I'll go through ya for a shortcut"

"Sure, ya wid'nt put a fox out aff a hen house that weather"

"Sure, they wid sickin ya, listing ta them"

"Aah sure you know yourself"

"They could talk the hind legs off a donkey"

"Sure the rain left me ringing wet"

"Dya ye know what I'm going ta tell ya"

"Sure, them ones are always giving out"

"Ah sure it'll be grand"

"Go-wan ya eegit ya"

"If there was work in the bed, they'd sleep on the floor"

"Sure, there's people dying today that never died before"

"It's absolutely cat mallojan"

"They're as mad as a box of frogs"

"What did I tell Ya"

"Wid ya have a titter a wit"

"De ya want a wee cuppa tae in yer han"

Sunday **01**

Aim to live life at the highest level

Let us not look back in anger, nor forward in fear, but around in awareness.

James Thurber

March

Great minds discuss ideas.
Average minds discuss events.
Small minds discuss people.

Eleanor Roosevelt

Don't give up. One day you'll look back and be glad you didn't.

Unknown

Monday **02**

Get creative

Tuesday **03**

Full Moon, Worm Moon

Adversity is a severe instructor

Wednesday **04**

Ask people's advice, but think for yourself

Thursday **05**

When you are stressed out, go for a long walk

Friday **06**

Make discipline an ally, not an enemy

Saturday **07**

Enjoy the day you're spending now

Sunday **08**

Start a regular savings-plan

Humour can alter any situation and help us cope at the very instant we are laughing.
Allen Klein

Life is hard. After all, it kills you.
Katharine Hepburn

March

Attitude is a little thing that makes a big difference.

Winston Churchill

One thing is certain in business, you and everyone around you will make mistakes.

Richard Branson

Monday 09

Treat everyone as you would a special guest

Tuesday 10

We all owe each other common courtesy

Wednesday 11

Laugh, laugh and laugh some more

Thursday **12**

Send love and forgiveness to everyone you know

Friday **13**

Kind deeds to others are an investment in yourself

Saturday **14**

Write a poem for somebody you care about

Sunday **15**

Mother's Day

Mother is your biggest cheerleader

**Knowledge comes from books.
Wisdom comes from life.**

*A busy mum is worth her
weight in gold.*

march

It's okay to pretend you're Irish on St Patricks Day. After all we all pretend, we're good at Christmas.

Rachel Handler

A little progress each day adds up to big results.

Satya Nani

Monday 16

It is never too late to say you're sorry

Tuesday 17

Happy St Patrick's Day!

Wishing you all the luck of the Irish

Wednesday 18

Keep your relationships loving and harmonious

New Moon   Thursday **19**

Choose to exercise regularly

Friday **20**

Life is a joy filled with delightful surprises

Saturday **21**

Pay your bills with a grateful heart

Sunday **22**

Honesty is the only policy

Irish Quote

Everything will be alright in the end.
If it's not alright
It's not the end.

march

*We didn't lose the game;
we just ran out of time.*

Vince Lombardi

*The quality of your
relationships determines
the quality of your life.*

E. Perel

Monday **23**

Kindness starts with a smile

Tuesday **24**

Write your thoughts down, start a Personal Journal

Wednesday **25**

Get enough sleep

Thursday **26**

Make a list of what bothers you

Friday **27**

Good ideas will not work unless you do

Saturday **28**

Be your own best friend

Summer Time Begins

Sunday **29**

Have a bath by candlelight

Irish Quote

May you get all your wishes but one, so you still have something to strive for.

March

The naked truth is always better than the best dressed lie.

Ann Landers

Age is of no importance unless you're a cheese.

Billie Burke

Monday **30**

Rejoice for the success and abundance of others

Tuesday **31**

Well begun is half done

I want to be able to say, that there are four things admirable for a woman to be, at any age! Whether you are four or forty-four or nineteen! It's always wonderful to be elegant, it's always fashionable to have grace, it's always glamorous to be brave, and it's always important to own a delectable perfume! Yes, wearing a beautiful fragrance is in style at any age!

C. JoyBell C.

SPRIOCANNA AIBREÁN

GOALS FOR APRIL

_____

_____

_____

_____

_____

_____

_____

_____

_____

_____

_____

An Irish Quote
There are no strangers here
Only friends you haven't yet met.
W.B. Yeats

Ní fiú bheith ag seanchas
agus an anachain déanta.

**No point in talking when
the damage is done.**

It is easy to halve the potato
where there is love.
Irish saying

April

Life is very short, so break your silly EGOS, forgive quickly, believe slowly, love truly, laugh loudly and never avoid anything that makes you smile.

Aradhya Lama

It's not enough to say you want to "lose weight" or "eat less and exercise more." It's too vague and doesn't give you a concrete target to work towards. You'll find it much easier to measure your success if you give yourself clearly defined targets to hit, such as:

- Go online to find seven recipes for quick and healthy meals to make for dinner this week.
- Go to a store and buy spinach, kale, peppers, sprouts, and radishes for lunch-time salads.
- Go for a two-mile walk or jog.
- Drink a green smoothie to offset craving for sweets.
- Eat veggies and homemade yogurt dip for today's afternoon snack.
- Avoid all foods with refined sugar or flour today.
- Drink herbal tea instead of wine tonight.
- Go to the gym at least for one hour every week
- Do 50 push-ups today.
- Avoid eating anything after 7pm.

Wednesday **01**

Be careful what you wish for

Full Moon, Pink Moon

Thursday 02

Visit someone old or lonely

Good Friday

Friday 03

Love your enemies

Saturday 04

You attract what you think about

Easter Sunday

Sunday 05

Easter is the time to spread peace, love and harmony

If you are not making mistakes, then you're not making decisions.
Cathrine Cook

Fashions fade, style is eternal.
Yves Saint-Laurent

April

An error doesn't become a mistake until you refuse to correct it.

Orlando A. Battista

I am a working woman with a secret life: I keep a house.

Cheryl Mendelson

Monday 06

Easter Monday

Plan a summer holiday

Tuesday 07

Speak evil of nobody

Wednesday 08

Bad money habits are serious

Thursday **09**

Start every day with a to-do list

Friday **10**

Review your daily actions before you go to sleep

Saturday **11**

Self-expression is essential to life

Sunday **12**

Dreamers are the saviours of the world

Mistakes are the growing pains of wisdom.
William George Jordan

Behind every great woman is another great woman.
Kate Hodges

April

Fear of making mistakes is just another way of procrastinating, of never moving forward.

Robin S Sharma

Other people's business is none of our business.

Monday 13

Get into a good book

Tuesday 14

Perseverance is faith in action

Wednesday 15

Cherish your ideals

Thursday **16**

Where there are true friends there is true wealth

New Moon

Friday **17**

Learn to dance

Saturday **18**

List your achievements

Sunday **19**

Great minds discuss ideas

**I can expect failure, but
I can't accept not trying.**

Michael Jordan

April

Invest in all the people who invest in you.

If it doesn't challenge you, it won't change you.

Monday 20

Look good even if you aren't going anywhere

Tuesday 21

Pack a bag of clothes for charity

Wednesday 22

De-clutter your life

Thursday **23**

Communicate with nature – even if you have to hug a tree!

Friday **24**

Those who follow the crowd are quickly lost in it

Saturday **25**

Surrender expectations

Sunday **26**

Visit an exhibition

Cooking with love provides food for the soul.

True Friends are the ones who have nice things to say about you behind your back.

Elbert Hubbard

April

A positive attitude causes a chain reaction of positive thought, events and outcomes. It is a catalyst, and it sparks extraordinary results.

Wade Boggs

Monday **27**

Start a container garden

Tuesday **28**

Don't jump to conclusions

Wednesday **29**

Associate with 'feel good' people, those who support you

Your Health Is Your Wealth

Ah your health is your wealth, now don't you forget it
These are the words my father told me
Back when I was a lad, such a long time ago
Your health is your wealth now I'm telling you so

It don't matter how rich with money you are
Or if you drive around in a big fancy car
If you're the Lord of the manor or the belle of the ball
If you haven't your health sure you've nothing at all

Ah your health is your wealth, now don't you forget it
These are the words my father told me
Back when I was a lad, such a long time ago
Your health is your wealth now I'm telling you so

You can have all your riches of diamonds or gold
But they don't mean nothing when the Lord takes your soul
But the one thing that will help you along every day
Is to stop, for a moment, and kneel down and pray

Ah your health is your wealth, now don't you forget it
These are the words my father told me
Back when I was a lad, such a long time ago
Your health is your wealth now I'm telling you so

Back when I was a lad, such a long time ago
Your health is your wealth now I'm telling you so.

Gerard Dornan

I used to be Snow White, but I drifted.

Mae West

The Little Things

It really is the little things
That mean the most of all...
The "let me help you with that" things
That may seem very small
The "I'll be glad to do it" things
That make your cares much lighter,
The "laugh with me, it's funny" things
That make your outlook brighter...

The "never mind the trouble" things,
The "yes, I understand,"
The interest and encouragement
In everything you've planned
It really is the little things,
The friendly word or smile,
That add such happiness to life
And make it more worthwhile

Mary Dawson Hughes

A bird doesn't sing
because it has an
answer, it sings
because it has
a song.

Maya Angelou

SPRIOCANNA

BEALTAINE

_____

_____

_____

_____

_____

_____

_____

_____

_____

_____

There's nothing so bad that it couldn't be worse.
Irish Proverb

If you have the words, there is always the chance that you'll find the way.
Seamus Heaney

Bíonn dhá insint ar gach aon scéal.
There are two sides to every story.

May

One way or another, our Karma will lead us to face ourselves.
We can look our karma in the eye, or we can wait for it to sneak up on us from behind.
One way or another, our karma will always find us...
No matter how hard we try, we can't escape our karma,
It follows us home.
I guess we can't really complain about karma.
It's not unfair. It's not unexpected. It just evens the score.
And even when we're about to do something we know will probably tempt karma to bite us in the back side, well, it goes without saying, we do it anyway.

George O'Malley

How you carry yourself speaks volumes about how you feel about yourself.

Cindy Ann Peterson

The ego relies on the familiar. It is reluctant to experience the unknown, which is the very essence of life.

Deepak Chopra

In a world that wants women to whisper, I choose to yell.

Luvvie Ajayi

Full Moon, Flower Moon

Friday 01

Love is not being possessive

Saturday 02

Be cautious with criticism

Sunday 03

Kindness has a ripple effect

A person's favourite sound is their name, so remember it.

Dale Carnegie

Dress well, no matter the occasion.

May

You never know how strong you are, until being strong is your only choice.

Bob Marley

When in doubt, wear red.

Bill Blass

Monday **04**   May Day

Never say 'no' to a gift

Tuesday **05**

Learn the gestures of love

Wednesday **06**

Dare to talk about your affections

Thursday **07**

Apologise when you're wrong

Friday **08**

Plant a herb garden

Saturday **09**

Treat yourself with kindness

Sunday **10**

Depend on yourself for your self-worth

Some people look for a beautiful place, others make a place beautiful.

Hazrat Inayat Khan

May

10% of conflict is due to a difference of opinion and 90% is due to the wrong tone of voice.
Na Mariz

Time spent with cats is never wasted.
Sigmund Freud

Monday 11

Make a friend feel special

Tuesday 12

Improve your roughage intake

Wednesday 13

Do a walking meditation

Thursday **14**

Your Health is EVERYTHING

Friday **15**

Humour and joy contribute to my well-being

New Moon

Saturday **16**

Step out of denial

Sunday **17**

Eat slowly and savour your food

Times are changing, you've got to change with the times.

Dominic Manetta

May

Success is not how high you have climbed, but how you make a positive difference to the world.

Roy T. Bennett

Monday **18**

Play 'hometown' tourist

Tuesday **19**

Say yes to Life

Wednesday **20**

Act how you would like to be

Thursday **21**

Plant a hanging basket

Friday **22**

Bake a cake this weekend

Saturday **23**

Stay curious

Sunday **24**

Learn to laugh at yourself

Never let a bad day make you feel like you have a bad life. Unknown

I learned the value of hard work by working hard. Margaret Mead

May

We lose ourselves in the things we love. We find ourselves there too.

Kristin Martz

Be comfortable on the open road.

Monday 25

Get some sunlight and fresh air

Tuesday 26

Work out disagreements

Wednesday 27

Grant people the freedom to be themselves

Thursday **28**

Grow flowers, the earth laughs in flowers

Friday **29**

Love the body you have

Saturday **30**

Share your knowledge

Full Blue Moon

Sunday **31**

Do less of what doesn't matter

The road to success is dotted with many tempting parking places. Will Rogers

God gives talent. Work transforms talent into genius. **Anna Pavlova**

DON'T

Don't wait for time. Make it.
Don't wait for love. Feel it.
Don't wait for money. Earn it.
Don't wait for a path to appear. Look for it.
Don't wait for opportunity. Find it.
Don't settle for less. Go for the best.
Don't compare. Be unique.
Don't fight your misfortune. Transform it.
Don't avoid failure. Learn from it.
Don't dwell on a mistake. Get over it.
Don't go back. Go around.
Don't close your eyes. Open your heart.
Don't run from life. Embrace it

Behind every working woman is an enormous pile of unwashed laundry.

Barbara Dale

But of course, I talk to myself, sometimes I need expert advice.

Edward Henheffer

People can't drive you crazy unless you give them the keys.

Dr. Mike Bechtle

If you are trying to be normal you will never know how amazing you can be.

Dr Maya Angelou

Dá fhad lá tagann oíche

As long as the day lasts, the night comes.

A good friend is like a four leaf clover, hard to find and lucky to have.

Irish proverb

There is no language like the Irish for soothing and quieting.

John Millington Synge
Irish Playwright

June

We are stronger, gentler, more resilient, and more beautiful than any of us imagine.

Mark Nepo

Those who mind don't matter, and those who matter don't mind.

Bernard M Baruch

Monday **01**	June Bank Holiday
	Finish what you've started

Tuesday **02**	
	Savour every moment

Wednesday **03**	
	Stay spiritually empowered

Thursday 04

Write a letter to someone

Friday 05

Remember to rest

Saturday 06

Nourish your friendships

Sunday 07

Use dreams for guidance

*I am not what happened to me,
I am what I choose to become.*

Carl Gustav Jung

June

Sometimes we build such high walls for protection that we forget that our greatest enemy can grow from within.

Eishes Chayil, Hush

If you can help it. never shake a hand while sitting down.

Monday 08

Cut down on sugar

Tuesday 09

Gaze at the moon and stars

Wednesday 10

Make peace with your past

Thursday 11

Manage information

Friday 12

Look for the open door

Saturday 13

Imagine the future

Sunday 14

The only person you can change is yourself

**And God said 'Love Your Enemy,'
and I obeyed him and loved myself.**

Kahlil Gibran

Wear sunscreen or a hat when outdoors

June

The point is not what we expect from life, but rather what life expects from us.

Viktor E. Frankl

Everything is changing. People are taking their comedians seriously and the politicians as a joke.

Will Rogers

Monday **15**	New Moon
	Pray for peace

Tuesday **16**	
	Take control of your surroundings

Wednesday **17**	
	*Have compassion for all beings*

Thursday **18**

Live within your means

Friday **19**

Temporary losses often result in permanent gain

Saturday **20**

Never act on impulse

Father's Day

Sunday **21**

Any man can be a father, but it takes someone special to be a dad

Being a great father is like shaving. No matter how good you shaved today, you have to do it again tomorrow.

Reed Markham

June

The more I live, the more I think that humour is the saving sense.

Jacob August Riis

Do not put each foot in a different boat.

Chinese Proverb

Monday 22

Dependability is the foundation of good character

Tuesday 23

Grace others with your cheerfulness

Wednesday 24

Do more of what makes you happy

Thursday **25**

Self-respect is the best way to get respect from others

Friday **26**

No one can keep you down but yourself

Saturday **27**

Independence starts with Self-dependence

Sunday **28**

Actions speak louder than words

**Every sunset is also a sunrise.
It all depends on where you
stand.**
                    Karl Schmidt

June

Listen to the wind, it talks.
Listen to the silence, it speaks.
Listen to your heart, it knows.

Native American Proverb

Each fresh peak ascended
teaches something.

Sir Martin Convay

Monday **29**

If you can't be right, be reasonable

Tuesday **30**   Full Moon, Strawberry Moon

Loyalty is the twin brother of Honesty

When you point the finger at someone else,
you should notice that three of your fingers
are pointing back at you.

Louis Nizer

Few things are more satisfying than seeing
your own children have teenagers of
their own.

Doug Larson

Get up and go diary 2026

Somewhere Over The Rainbow

Somewhere over the rainbow,
Way up high,
There's a land that I heard of
Once in a lullaby.
Somewhere over the rainbow
Skies are blue,
And the dreams that you dare to dream
Really do come true.
Some days I'll wish upon a star
And wake up where the clouds are far behind me,
Where troubles melt like lemon drops
Way above the chimney pots,
That's where you'll find me.
Somewhere over the rainbow
Bluebirds fly.
If birds fly over the rainbow
Why then, oh why can't I?
If happy little blue birds fly beyond the rainbow,
Why, oh why, can't I?

from The Wizard of Oz

I no longer have patience for certain things, not because I've become arrogant, but simply because I reached a point in my life where I do not want to waste more time with what displeases me or hurts me. I have no patience for cynicism, excessive criticism and demands of any nature. I lost the will to please those who do not like me, to love those who do not love me and to smile at those who do not want to smile at me. I no longer spend a single minute on those who lie or want to manipulate. I decided not to coexist anymore with pretence, hypocrisy, dishonesty and cheap praise. I do not tolerate selective erudition nor academic arrogance. I do not adjust either to popular gossiping. I hate conflict and comparisons. I believe in a world of opposites and that's why I avoid people with rigid and inflexible personalities. In friendship I dislike the lack of loyalty and betrayal. I do not get along with those who do not know how to give a compliment or a word of encouragement. Exaggerations bore me and I have difficulty accepting those who do not like animals. And on top of everything I have no patience for anyone who does not deserve my patience.

Meryl Streep

The Power Of One

One song can spark a moment,
One whisper can wake the dream.
One tree can start a forest,
One bird can herald spring.

One smile begins a friendship,
One moment can make one fall in luv.
One star can guide a ship at sea,
One word can frame the goal

One vote can change a nation,
One sunbeam lights a room
One candle wipes out darkness,
One laugh will conquer gloom.

One step must start each journey.
One word must start each prayer.
One hope will raise our spirits,
One touch can show you care.

One voice can speak with wisdom,
One heart can know what's true,
One life can make a difference,
You see, it's up to you!

Author Unknown

Choose a job you love, and you will never have to work a day in your life.

Confucius

Success is the sum of small efforts, repeated day in and day out.

R. Collier

Best way to get rid of kitchen odours: Eat out.

Phyllis Diller

I learned to always take on things I'd never done before. Growth and comfort do not coexist.

Virginia Rometty

GOALS FOR JULY

_____
_____
_____
_____
_____
_____
_____
_____
_____
_____

Ireland is like no other place under heaven.
George Bernard Shaw

With freedom, books, flowers, and the moon, who could not be happy?
Oscar Wilde

Glacann fear críonna comhairle.

A wise man takes advice.

July

Don't worry about failure,
Worry about the chances you miss when
you don't even try.

Jack Canfield

Greatness is your
potential. Action is
your opportunity.

John C. Maxwell

At the end of a matter ask,
"What will I learn from this
to make me better?"

Mary Anne Radmacher

Never carry
more cash than
you can afford
to lose.

Protect who is
behind you and
respect who is
beside you.

Wednesday **01**

Someone that you don't even know exists, may love you

Thursday **02**

Find peace in whatever you do

Friday **03**

Be your own person

Saturday **04**

Try a calming activity

Sunday **05**

Light a scented candle

YOU GET WHAT YOU GIVE

When one door closes in your life, nail it up and move on.

July

Science is organised knowledge.
Wisdom is organised life.

Immanuel Kant

Make the most of
yourself… for that is
all there is of you.

Ralph Waldo Emerson

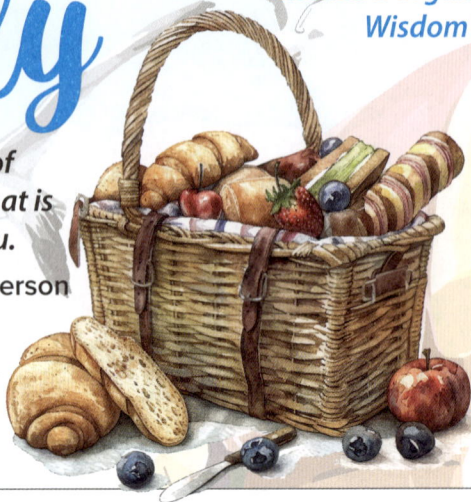

When preparing
to climb a
mountain, pack
a light heart.

Dan May

Monday 06

Care for your inner child

Tuesday 07

Don't worry about that which you cannot control

Wednesday 08

Improve your posture

Thursday **09**

Eat three balanced meals per day

Friday **10**

Your children get only one childhood

Saturday **11**

Every little choice you make counts

Sunday **12**

Make your loved ones feel good about themselves

I can be changed by what happens to me. But I refuse to be reduced by it.

Maya Angelou

July

Speak honestly: say what you think and mean what you say.

George S. Patton

The best networking strategy is a helping others first strategy.

Nick Fox

Monday **13**

You attract the things you fear

Tuesday **14**   New Moon

Let go of resentment and regret.

Wednesday **15**

Light a candle for somebody

Thursday 16

Choose not to be a victim

Friday 17

Hug well, hug often

Saturday 18

Expect the best

Sunday 19

Dance with life – curve, bend and blend

If you really want to do something,
You will find a way.
If you don't you will find an excuse.

Jim Rohn

July

Don't take the credit for work you didn't do.

When I'm worried and I can't sleep I count my blessings instead of sheep.
Irving Berlin

Don't take anything personally. Nothing others do is because of you.
Miguel Angel Ruiz

Monday 20

Observe moderation and balance in all things

Tuesday 21

Listen to the sound of silence

Wednesday 22

Never take anything for granted

Thursday **23**

Always be truthful, and under all conditions

Friday **24**

Listen with courtesy to what others say

Saturday **25**

Hatred is the archenemy of happiness

Sunday **26**

Let humour soften your journey

A compromise is an agreement whereby both parties get what neither of them wanted.
Joseph Andrus

July

Instead of believing that you know what's good for others, trust that they know what's good for themselves.

Unknown

Life is not a matter of holding good cards, but sometimes, playing a poor hand well.

Jack London

Monday **27**

From small beginnings come great things

Tuesday **28**

Do the important things before they become urgent

Wednesday **29**   Full Moon, Buck Moon

Be willing to compromise

Thursday **30**

Love your work

Friday **31**

Buy yourself an ice cream today

You can't go back and
change the beginning,
But you can start where you
are and change the ending.

C. S. Lewis

TEENAGERS
TIRED of being
harassed by your
parents?

ACT NOW
Move out, get a job,
pay your own bills
While you still know
EVERYTHING.

*May every sunrise hold
more promise, and every
sunset hold more peace.*

Umair Siddiqui

You don't get what
you wish for.
You get what you
work for.

Danial Milstein

In the midst of movement and chaos, keep stillness inside of you.

Deepak Chopra

The practice of forgiveness is our most important contribution to the healing of the world..

Marianne Williamson

Get your thoughts in order – write them down.

The only one who can tell you' you can't win is you, and you don't have to listen.

Jessica Ennis

Give the world the best you have, and the best will come back to you.

Madeline Bridges

You don't have to see the whole staircase, just take the first step.

Martin Luther King, Jr.

To see happiness in action, Smile and start a chain reaction.

SPRIOCANNA

GOALS FOR AUGUST

LÚNASA

_____
_____
_____
_____
_____
_____
_____
_____
_____
_____
_____

Is deacair ceann críonna a chur ar cholainn óg.

It's difficult to put a wise head on young shoulders.

May the saddest day of your future be no worse than the happiest day of your past.
Irish Blessing

You know its summer in Ireland when the rain gets warmer.
Hal Roach, Irish Comedian

August

He who bemoans the lack of opportunity, forgets small doors many times open up into large rooms.

Rubin Hurricane Carter

Never put off until tomorrow what you can do today.
Never trouble another for what you can do yourself.
Never spend money before you have it.
Never buy what you do not want because it is cheap.
We seldom repent having eaten too little.
Nothing is troublesome that we do willingly.
How much pain the worries have cost us that never happened!
Take things always by the smooth handle.
When angry always count to ten before you speak
If very angry a hundred backwards.

If I Had My Child To Rear Again

If I had my child to raise all over again,
I'd finger-paint more and point the finger less
I'd do less correcting and more connecting.
I'd take my eyes off my watch and watch with my eyes.
I would care to know less and know to care more.
I'd take more hikes and fly more kites.
I'd stop playing serious and seriously play.
I'd run through more fields and gaze at more stars.
I'd do more hugging and less tugging.
I would be firm less often and affirm much more.
I'd build self-esteem first, and the house later.
I'd teach less about the love of power,
and more about the power of love.

Rubin Hurricane Carter

Saturday **01**

Whatever you do, do it well

Sunday **02**

Visit your local library

When you destroy someone's life with lies, take it as a loan, it will come back to you with interest.

Unknown

August

Friends are those rare people who ask how we are and then wait to hear the answer.

Ed Cunningham

The one who has a heart full of love always has something to give.

Pope John XXIII

Monday **03**	August Bank Holiday
	Make a 'bucket list'

Tuesday **04**	
	If you bring sunshine to others it will reflect in you

Wednesday **05**	
	Today's hopes become tomorrow's realities

Thursday 06

Practice to communicate warmth

Friday 07

Harmony with self leads to harmony with others

Saturday 08

Don't borrow trouble

Sunday 09

Give someone a pleasant surprise

**You can't have everything.
Where would you put it?**

Mark Twain

**The best way out is
always through.**

Robert Frost

Get up and go diary 2026

91

August

Remember no human condition is ever permanent. Then you will not be overjoyed in good fortune or too sorrowful in your misfortune.

Socrates

Monday **10**

Faith never diminishes through use

Tuesday **11**

Get your affairs in order

Wednesday **12**   New Moon

Courage is one jump ahead of fear

Thursday **13**

Explore herbal remedies

Friday **14**

Feed the plants in your garden

Saturday **15**

Give a sincere compliment to everyone you talk to today

Sunday **16**

Notice the beauty of small moments

Dost, thou love life? Then do not squander time;
For that's the stuff life is made of.

Benjamin Franklin

August

Progress is impossible without change, and those who cannot change their minds cannot change anything.

George Bernard Shaw

Monday **17**

Pick some wildflowers

Tuesday **18**

To love oneself is the beginning of a lifelong romance

Wednesday **19**

Keep your appointments

Thursday **20**

Play, play and play some more

Friday **21**

Barter, exchange and buy together

Saturday **22**

Have a family dinner

Sunday **23**

Keep a schedule

A bend in the road is not the end of the road… unless you fail to make the turn.

Helen keller

Enjoy the beauty of a sunset, nature's kiss for the night.

Sharon Rene

August

A great voyage is a journey that never ends.

Pat Conroy

A good listener is not only popular everywhere, but after a while he knows something.

Wilson Mizner

Monday **24**

Decide to be healthy

Tuesday **25**

Give up 'people pleasing'

Wednesday **26**

Create positive habits

Thursday **27**

Give gifts of service

Full Moon, Sturgeon Moon

Friday **28**

Arrange some flowers for your living room

Saturday **29**

Don't put off something you have always wanted to do

Sunday **30**

Learn about your chakras

Rowing harder doesn't help if your boat is headed in the wrong direction.

Kenichi Ohmae

Everything is funny, as long as it's happening to somebody else.

Will Rogers

August

I am instantly 70% nicer after 3pm on Fridays.

Unknown

Every time you talk your mind is on parade.

Samuel Johnson

Monday **31**

Keep a coin jar

Wee Hughie

He's gone to school, Wee Hughie,
an' him not four.
Sure I saw the fright was in him
When he left the door.

But he took a hand o' Denny
an' a hand o' Dan,
Wi' Joe's owld coat upon him –
Och, the poor wee man!

He cut the quarest figure,
More stout nor thin;
An' trottin' right an' steady
Wi his toes turned in.

I watched him to the corner
0' the big turf stack,
An' the more his feet went forrit,
Still his head turned back.

He was lookin',
would I call him –
Och me heart was woe-
Sure it's lost I am without him,
But he be to go.

I followed to the turnin'
When they passed it by,
God help him, he was cryin',
An', maybe, so was I.

Elizabeth Shane 1877 -1951

SPRIOCANNA

MEÁN FOMHAIR

_____
_____
_____
_____
_____
_____
_____
_____
_____
_____

Being Irish, he had an abiding sense of tragedy, which sustained him through temporary periods of joy.

William Butler Yeats

Is fearr an tsláinte ná na táinte.

Health is better than wealth.

September

Healthy Bread

- 2 cups of whole wheat flour
- 1 cup of breakfast oats
- 2 teaspoons bicarbonate of soda
- 2 teaspoons of baking powder
- ¼ cup sugar
- 500 ml buttermilk

Mix the first 5 ingredients
Add the buttermilk
Mix very well
Bake in a greased, floured
    bread baking tin.
Bake at 180°C for 45 minutes.

Tuesday 01

Bake your own bread

Wednesday 02

Take care of social obligations

Thursday 03

Reflect on the good memories of your childhood

Friday 04

True love is generous in spirit

Saturday 05

Be thankful and cheerful

Sunday 06

Play to win, but be a good loser

One of the most courageous decisions you will ever make is to finally let go of whatever is hurting your heart and soul.

Brigitte Nicole

September

Extraordinary people survive under the most terrible circumstances and they become more extraordinary because of it.
Robertson Davies

Freedom is nothing but a chance to be better.
Albert Camus

Monday **07**

Accept whatever life throws at you, choose to act

Tuesday **08**

Don't assume the feelings of others

Wednesday **09**

Be done with those who continue to hurt you

Thursday 10

Act toward your goals

New Moon

Friday 11

Everybody deserves to be loved

Saturday 12

Release the resentment and anger

Sunday 13

Turn on happy music and dance

You and I are all as much continuous with the physical universe as a wave is continuous with the ocean.

Alan Watts

September

Having a place to go is a home.
Having someone to love is a family.
Having both is a blessing.

Donna Hedges

We often take for granted the very
things that most deserve our gratitude.

Cynthia Ozick

Monday **14**

Spend some time with a furry friend

Tuesday **15**

Forgive someone for something

Wednesday **16**

Stretch your body

Thursday **17**

Don't impose your values on others

Friday **18**

Be grateful for all of life

Saturday **19**

Enjoy the process of reaching your healthy weight

Sunday **20**

Forgive yourself for past mistakes

Strength does not come from physical capacity. It comes from an indomitable will.

Mahatma Ghandi

Peace of mind calls for a clear conscience.

September

An optimist is one who makes the best of what he gets the worst of.

Anon

Awareness is the first step in healing.

Dean Ornish

An apology is a good way to have the last word.

Unknown

Monday **21**

You deserve health, energy and calmness

Tuesday **22**

You are strong and resourceful

Wednesday **23**

Balance self-confidence with modesty

Thursday **24**

Everything in life matters

Friday **25**

Be motivated by both successes and failures

Full Moon, Harvest Moon

Saturday **26**

There is no need to ever tolerate disrespect

Sunday **27**

Get up early

When you are playing in the game of life, be a good sport.

Nothing can bring you peace but yourself.

Ralph waldo Emerson

September

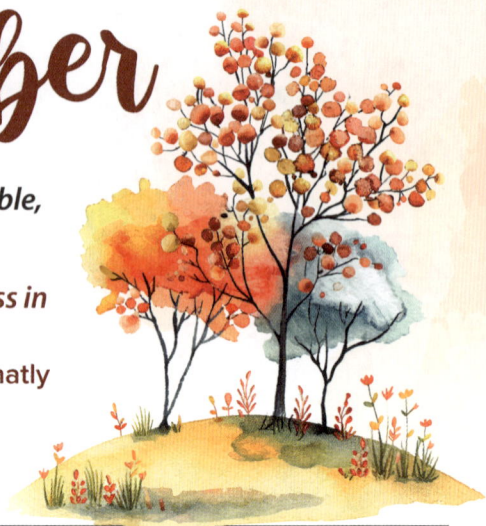

It is better to go forward and stumble, than to sit idle and grumble.

Never put the key to your happiness in someone else's pocket.

Dr Lori Whatly

Life, if well lived, is long enough.
Seneca

Monday **28**

Cultivate a positive mental attitude

Tuesday **29**

Make a list of "un-done's" and start doing them

Wednesday **30**

Only YOU can get
YOUR health checked

Watch a 'feel good' movie

SPRIOCANNA

DEIREADH FOMHAIR

_____

_____

_____

_____

_____

_____

_____

_____

_____

Is olc an ghaoth nach séideann do dhuine éigin.

It's an ill wind blows nobody any good.

Take up your responsibilities and be prepared to go your own way depending for safety on your own courage, your own truth and your own common sense.

Constance Markievicz

October

The Greatest ...

The most satisfying work ... Helping Others
The most endangered species ... Dedicated Leaders
The greatest natural resource ... Our Youth
The greatest shot in the arm ... Encouragement
The greatest problem to overcome ... Fear
The most effective sleeping pill ... Peace of Mind
The most crippling failure disease ... Excuses
The most powerful force in life ... Love
The world's most incredible computer ... The Brain
The worst thing to be without ... Hope
The most powerful relationship tool ... The Tongue
The two most power-filled words ... "I Can"
The most powerful communication ... Prayer
The greatest asset ... Faith
The most worthless emotion ... Self-pity
The most prized possession ... Self-esteem
The most contagious spirit ... Enthusiasm
The most beautiful attire ... SMILE

You arrived naked. You will pass out naked.
You arrived without goods or money.
You will also leave without goods or money.
Your first bath? Someone has washed you.
Your last bath? Someone will wash you.
This is life
So why all the malice? Why so much envy?
Why so much hate? Why so much resentment?
Why so much selfishness?
Be good to each other. Do the right things.
We have limited time on earth.
Do not waste it on useless things.

Unknown

Thursday 01

Life's burdens are lighter when you can laugh at yourself

Friday 02

You aren't supposed to be perfect

Saturday 03

There are reasons to smile all around you

Sunday 04

Tough times help us grow

A wise person once said
"Be careful who you let on board,
because some people will sink the
whole ship just because they can't
be the captain.

October

You are the C.E.O. of your life. Hire, fire and promote accordingly. Accept people as they are but place them where they belong.

Todd Hayes

Life lives; life dies. life laughs, life cries.
Life gives up and again life tries.
Life looks different through everyone's eyes.

Monday **05**

Repetition is not failure

Tuesday **06**

No matter what, you have a purpose

Wednesday **07**

Being true to yourself is always the best option

Thursday 08

Right now, is a fresh start

Friday 09

You don't always have to be happy and cheerful

New Moon

Saturday 10

It's okay to let some things go

Sunday 11

Work hard on the essential

The secret of genius is to carry the spirit of the child into old age, which means never losing your enthusiasm.
Aldous Huxley

October

Folks are usually about as happy as they make up their minds to be.

Abraham Lincoln

Autumn, the Beautiful Time of Year Between Heat Stroke and Frost Bite.

Monday **12**

Nurture your self-confidence

Tuesday **13**

Focus on solutions

Wednesday **14**

Balance work with necessary rest

Thursday 15

Set a good example

Friday 16

Kindness in thinking creates positivity

Saturday 17

True love is always shown in deeds, not words

Sunday 18

Help change one life

Life isn't as serious as sometimes our minds make it out to be.
Eckhart Tolle

Some family trees bear an enormous crop of nuts.
Wayne Huizenga

October

Those who know do not speak. Those who speak do not know.

Lao Tzu

Your belief in any idea will give life to it.

Mooji

Monday **19**

Start spending time with the right people

Tuesday **20**

Give new people you meet a chance

Wednesday **21**

Cheer for other people's victories

Thursday **22**

Listen to your own inner voice

Friday **23**

Be attentive to your stress level and take short breaks

Saturday **24**

Say what you need to say to whom you need to say it

Sunday **25**

Actively nurture your most important relationships

Our best successes often come after our greatest disappointments.

Henry Ward Beecher

Praise publicly. Criticise privately.

Warren Buffett

October

You'd be surprised how uncommon common sense really is.

Alan T. Amato

I feel more and more the time wasted that is not spent in Ireland.

Lady Gregory

Monday **26**	Full Moon, Hunter's Moon. October Bank Holiday

Keep work at work

Tuesday **27**	

Accept and embrace change

Wednesday **28**	

Don't try to please everyone

Thursday **29**

Be more open about how you feel

Friday **30**

Worry less about what others think about you

Saturday **31**

Have a dinner by candlelight

If you don't have a costume yet, don't worry, you can always dress up as yourself.

If You've Got It, Haunt It!

Broom Parking Only.

Come in for a Spell.

Witches Get Stitches

Tis the Season to Be Spooky

May your days be scary and bright!

October

Dare to Be...

When a new day begins, dare to smile gratefully.
When there is darkness, dare to be the first to shine a light.
When there is injustice, dare to be the first to condemn it.
When something seems difficult, dare to do it anyway.
When life seems to beat you down, dare to fight back.
When there seems to be no hope, dare to find some.
When you're feeling tired, dare to keep going.
When times are tough, dare to be tougher. When love hurts you, dare to love again.
When someone is hurting, dare to help them heal.
When another is lost, dare to help them find the way.
When a friend falls, dare to be the first to extend a hand.
When you cross paths with another, dare to make them smile.
When you feel great, dare to help someone else feel great too.
When the day has ended, dare to feel as you've done your best.
Dare to be the best you can –
At all times, Dare to be!

Steve Maraboli

Grief never ends...
But it changes.
It's a passage,
not a place to stay.
Grief is not a
sign of weakness,
nor a lack of faith...
It is the price of love.

Elizabeth I

Life's tragedy is that
we get old too soon
and wise too late.

Benjamin Franklin

_____

_____

_____

_____

_____

_____

_____

As a child my family's menu consisted of two choices: take it or leave it.

Buddy Hackett

MENU CHOICES
1. *Take it* ☐
2. *Leave it* ☐

Taithí a dhéanann máistreacht.

Practice makes perfect.

November

Usually, time takes a flight when we are enjoying ourselves, but we all have got the same amount of time.

60 seconds in 1 minute
3600 seconds in 1hour
86400 seconds in1 day
604800 seconds in 1 week
2628002 seconds in 1 month
31.536,000 seconds in 1 year
1 billion seconds in 31.71 years
1 trillion seconds in 31709.80 years
Do not waste 1 second

The meaning of things lies not in the thing themselves, but in our attitude towards them.

Antoine de Saint - Exupery

Three things never come back – Time, Words and Opportunity. Therefore: do not waste time, Choose your words, do not miss the opportunity.

Confucius

Wisdom has two parts:
1. *Knowing what to say.*
2. *Not saying it...*

It's never too late to make things right.

Unknown

Self-love

Take full responsibility for your life.
Stop blaming others.
See yourself as the cause of what happens to you.
Do things you like to do.
Don't stay in a job you don't like.
Participate in life at the highest level you can.
Watch what you say. Avoid self-put-downs.
Stop being critical of yourself and others.
Take care of your body. Give it exercise and good food.
Be willing to create a lifestyle that generates and nourishes self-esteem.
Associate with others with high esteem.
Stop trying to change others.
Focus your attention on being the way you want others to be.
Acknowledge others frequently.
Tell them what you like and appreciate in them.

I believe in angels, The kind
heaven sends,
I am surrounded by angels,
But I call them friends.

Unknown

Sunday **01**

Engage yourself in a meaningful personal project

You are not only responsible for what you say, but also for what you do not say.

Martin Luther

Nothing lasts forever. Not even your troubles.

Arnold H Glasgow

November

Worrying never fixes anything.
Ernest Hemingway

Dress well, no matter the occasion.

Friday is my second favourite F word. Food is my first!
Unknown

Monday **02**

Follow through with a promise

Tuesday **03**

Feed the birds

Wednesday **04**

Don't confuse foolishness with bravery

Thursday **05**

The future depends on what you do today

Friday **06**

Celebrate everything you can

Saturday **07**

Turn off the computer and connect with people

Sunday **08**

Express your needs and feelings

Even the smallest grain of rice will tip the scales.

We realise the importance of our voices only when we are silenced.

Malala Yousafzai

November

It's never too late to take a moment to look.

Sharon Salzberg

Don't wish your days away, waiting for better ones ahead.

Marjorie Pay Hinckly

Monday **09**	New Moon
	Live and let live

Tuesday **10**	
	Plan a get-together with friends

Wednesday **11**	
	Do ordinary things in an extraordinary way

Thursday **12**

Within you are so many answers

Friday **13**

Allow the universe to guide you

Saturday **14**

Never speak badly about yourself

Sunday **15**

Isolation leads to self-confrontation

Never talk bad about food when you are the guest.

Out of difficulties grow miracles.
Marjorie Pay Hinckly

November

Never trouble another for what you can do yourself.

Whatever is worth doing at all is worth doing well.

It's not fair to ask others what you are not willing to do yourself.

Monday 16

Less means more

Tuesday 17

If you want people to like you, like them first

Wednesday 18

Your future depends on your dreams

Thursday **19**

Cherish your ideals

Friday **20**

Today's hopes become tomorrow's realities

Saturday **21**

Create, connect, convert

Sunday **22**

Time, Words, Opportunity -
Once gone, never come back

Laziness may appear attractive,
but work gives you satisfaction

It's a terrible burden,
having nothing to do.

November

You

You are brave. You are enough. Your words are meaningful.
You have great Ideas. You are the best at being you.
You are beautiful inside and out. You are interesting.
You can say yes. You can say no. You are loved. You are worth it.
Don't be afraid of yourself. We all make mistakes.
You don't have to be perfect to be great. It is ok to cry.
Self-care is important. You are not anyone's expectations.
Thank you for being you.

Unknown

Monday **23**

Life is a journey to be savoured every step of the way

Tuesday **24**   Full Moon, Beaver Moon

'One day' is far away

Wednesday **25**

Only the weak crave sympathy

Happy Thanksgiving

Thursday 26

Everything happens for a reason

Friday 27

Struggle is a choice. Choose joy instead

Saturday 28

Be generous and helpful

Sunday 29

There is more pleasure in giving than there is in receiving

The time to relax is when you don't have time for it.

Sydney J. Harris

November

Excellence is not a skill it's an attitude.

Ralph Marston

Part of the healing process is sharing with other people who care.

Jerry Cantrell

Monday **30**

Be willing to share your blessings

Irish Philosophy

*There are only two things to worry about
either you are well, or you are sick.
If you are well then there is nothing to worry about.
But if you are sick, then there are two things to worry
about, either you will get well or you will die.
If you get well, there is nothing to worry about.
If you die, then there are only two things to worry
about, either you will go to heaven or hell.
If you go to heaven, there is nothing to worry about.
But if you go to hell, You'll be so damn busy shaking
hands with friends you won't have time to worry.*

WHY WORRY

SPRIOCANNA NOLLAIG

_____

_____

_____

_____

_____

_____

_____

_____

_____

An rud nach féidir ní féidir é.

What cannot be done, cannot be done.

I only take a drink on two occasions - when I am thirsty and when I am not.

Brendan Behan

December

When you love what you have, you have everything you need.

A.A. Milne

Difference is the essence of humanity. Difference is an accident of birth, and it should therefore never be the source of hatred or conflict.
The answer to the difference is to respect it.
Therein lies a most fundamental principle of peace: respect for diversity.

John Hume

A good teacher is like a candle - it consumes itself to light the way for others.

Mustafa Kemal Atatürk

Tuesday **01**

Overcome a fear

Wednesday **02**

Don't be the person to fan the flames

Thursday 03

Money can't buy the unconditional love of a child

Friday 04

Develop your talents – everybody is good at something

Saturday 05

Love conquers all

Sunday 06

Simplicity brings calm

Some people come into your life as blessings, others come into your life as lessons.

Mother Teresa

December

Rejoice with your family in the beautiful land of life.
Albert Einstein

True friends are those rare people who come to find you in dark places and lead you back to the light.
Steven Aitchison

Live well, love much, laugh often.
Bessie Anderson Stanley

Monday **07**

Cherish your ideals

Tuesday **08**

Start your Christmas shopping before it gets crowded

Wednesday **09**   New Moon

Forget your past failures and focus on your future successes

Thursday **10**

Curiosity will always lead you down a new path

Friday **11**

Think of kind gestures as gifts

Saturday **12**

Dreamers are the saviours of the world

Sunday **13**

Be open to the possibility of miracles

Asking is the beginning of receiving. Make sure you don't go to the ocean with a teaspoon.

Jim Rohn - 1930-2009
Author and Speaker

December

Our peace shall stand as firm as rocky mountains.

William Shakespeare

When a friend falls, dare to be the first to extend a helping hand.

Steve Maraboli

Monday **14**

Get out of your head and do something

Tuesday **15**

You attract what you fear

Wednesday **16**

Follow the principle of live and let live

Thursday **17**

You are kind, loving and unafraid

Friday **18**

As you forgive yourself, it becomes easier to forgive others

Saturday **19**

Be Forgiving and Kind

Sunday **20**

A family is a strong support network

Hearts are not to be had as a gift, hearts are to be earned.

W. B. Yeats

December

A Christmas Blessing

During this Christmas season,
May you be blessed with the spirit of the
season which is peace.
The gladness of the season which is hope.
And the heart of the season which is love.

Irish Christmas Blessing

Monday **21**

Choose with an open mind and an open heart

Tuesday **22**

Look for the silver lining

Wednesday **23**

Take things always by the smooth handle

Cold Moon / Super Full Moon   Thursday **24**

Its Christmas eve; Enjoy a silent night

Christmas Day   Friday **25**

HAVE A WONDERFUL CHRISTMAS.

the get up and go team

Celebrate Your Blessings

St. Stephen's Day   Saturday **26**

Enjoy a do-nothing day

Sunday **27**

Give your left-over Christmas delights to the needy

---

*He who has not Christmas
in his heart will not find it
under the Christmas tree.*

Roy L. Smith

December

Your children need your PRESENCE more than your PRESENTS.

Jesse Jackson

Christmas is most truly Christmas when we celebrate it by giving the light of love to those who need it most.

Ruth Carter Stapleton

Monday **28**

Happiness is made of 'little things'

Tuesday **29**

You make a difference, you are worthy

Wednesday **30**

Make a list of short and long-term goals

New Year's Eve

What is your number 1 New Year resolution?

The future lies before you like a field of fallen snow, be careful how you tread on it for every step will show.

Doris A. Wright

If you don't stand for something, you will fall for anything.

Gordon Eadie

Desiderata

Go placidly amid the noise and haste and remember what peace there may be in silence. As far as possible without surrender be on good terms with all persons. Speak your truth quietly and clearly, and listen to others, even the dull and ignorant; they too have their story.

Avoid loud and aggressive persons, they are vexations to the spirit. If you compare yourself with others, you may become vain and bitter; for always there will be greater and lesser persons than yourself. Enjoy your achievements as well as your plans.

Keep interested in your own career, however humble; it is a real possession in the changing fortunes of time. Exercise caution in your business affairs; for the world is full of trickery. But let this not blind you to what virtue there is; many persons strive for high ideals; and everywhere life is full of heroism.

Be yourself. Especially, do not feign affection. Neither be cynical about love; for in the face of all aridity and disenchantment it is perennial as the grass.

Take kindly the counsel of the years, gracefully surrendering the things of youth. Nurture strength of spirit to shield you in sudden misfortune. But do not distress yourself with imaginings.Many fears are born of fatigue and loneliness. Beyond a wholesome discipline, be gentle with yourself.

You are a child of the universe, no less than the trees and the stars; you have a right to be here. And whether or not it is clear to you, no doubt the universe is unfolding as it should.

Therefore, be at peace with God, whatever you conceive Him to be; and whatever your labours and aspirations, in the noisy confusion of life keep peace with your soul.

With all its sham, drudgery and broken dreams, it is still a beautiful world. Be cheerful.

Strive to be happy.

Max Ehrmann

NOTES

NOTES

NOTES

**TO SEE OUR FULL RANGE OF DIARIES AND JOURNALS,
PLEASE VISIT OUR WEBSITE:**

www.getupandgodiary.com

**GetUpandGo
Publications**
WE ASPIRE TO INSPIRE

CONTACT US

Post: Get Up and Go Publications Ltd,
Unit 7A Cornhill Business Park, Ballyshannon,
Co Donegal, Ireland F94 H52

Email: info@getupandgodiary.com
Tel: 071 98 45938 or 085 1764297 (office hours)

- -

ORDER FORM

The Irish Get Up and Go Diary (paperback), €12.95/£11	Quantity	
The Irish Get Up and Go Diary (padded cover), €18.50/£16	Quantity	
The Get Up and Go Diary (paperback), €12.95/£11	Quantity	
Get Up and Go Diary for Busy Women (paperback), €12.95/£11	Quantity	
Get Up and Go Diary for Busy Women (padded cover), €18.50/£16	Quantity	
Get up and Go Young Person's Diary €12.95/£11	Quantity	
Daily Guide to Good Health and Wellbeing (paperback), €16.50/£14	Quantity	
Get Up and Go Gratitude Journal (padded cover), €18.50/£16	Quantity	
Get Up and Go Wallplanner (size: A1), €4/£4	Quantity	
	Total number of copies	

ADD POSTAGE AND PACKING

Standard postage for 1/2 Paperback Diaries Anywhere in Ireland: €3.50
1 Paperback Diary To Great Britain & Europe: €5.95, USA/CAN: €9.50 Aus/NZ: €11.50
For bulk postage and tracking rates please refer to our website or call +353 85 1764297

I enclose cheque/postal order for (total amount including P+P):_____

Name: _____

Address: _____

Post Code: _____ Phone no: _____

Email:_____

**To pay by credit/debit card or with any other queries
please contact us 071 98 45938 or 085 1764297 during office hours**